PLANE ACTION

Written by Shweta Bahri and Keya Lamba
Illustrated by James Gibbs

activist: an activist is someone who works to change the world around them and inspires others to do the same

OXFORD
UNIVERSITY PRESS

Words to look out for . . .

advise *(verb)*
advises, advising, advised
To advise someone is to tell them what you think they should do.

analyse *(verb)*
analyses, analysing, analysed
to think carefully about something, or look carefully at something, considering each part in detail

assortment *(noun)*
a mixture of different things or people

detach *(verb)*
detaches, detaching, detached
To detach something is to remove it or separate it.

exceed *(verb)*
exceeds, exceeding, exceeded
to be bigger, better, or more than something

inaccurate *(adjective)*
not correct

justify *(verb)*
justifies, justifying, justified
to show or say that something is right, fair or reasonable

reassure *(verb)*
reassures, reassuring, reassured
to say or do something that makes someone feel less worried

represent *(verb)*
represents, representing, represented

1. to be an example of something

2. to act or speak on someone's behalf

undermine *(verb)*
undermines, undermining, undermined
To undermine a plan, a person or their efforts is to make them less effective.

Contents

Earth's crisis

Hi! My name is Dr Maya and I'm a climate scientist. I work to find possible solutions to the world's greatest crisis.

Our beautiful home, Planet Earth, is facing its biggest ever challenge: climate change.

What's the big problem?

Have you heard about climate change – but wondered why everyone's talking about it?

The climate on our planet has always changed, but slowly. It's now changing much more quickly, due to things humans do.

The main reason for climate change is burning **fossil fuels** like coal and oil.

Burning fossil fuels releases gases like **carbon dioxide**.

These gases trap heat around Earth.

Trapped heat causes temperatures to rise. This can cause extreme weather, harm wildlife, and make it hard to get food and water.

For all those reasons, climate change is now a threat to our planet and our future.

So, where do climate scientists like me fit in? We …

- study changes in Earth's **atmosphere**, oceans and land
- find evidence for what causes climate change and what **impact** it has
- design computer programs to explore these impacts.

We also work on creating new solutions to tackle climate change. Some amazing ones have already been invented …

Electric cars

- Electric cars run on batteries, not petrol.
- They create less carbon **emissions**, if the electricity that charges their batteries doesn't come from fossil fuels.

Carbon capture technology

- These machines remove carbon from the air.
- The captured carbon is buried in the ground or used to make new products.

Technology to predict the weather

- **Artificial intelligence** (AI) collects information to help predict extreme events like wildfires.
- It can also help people track how much energy they use.

Climate inventors and change-makers

Other inventions have been created by young people from all over the world.

Many young people have experienced extreme weather events that caused terrible damage to their homes. Many have seen their local environment harmed and wildlife threatened.

In response, some of them took **innovative** action to find solutions to the crisis. Their stories and inventions are seriously impressive.

In this book, you'll read motivating true stories of some passionate young heroes taking inventive action to protect our planet.

Their actions have inspired their communities to unite and create a better world. They have demonstrated that even the most challenging problems can be solved if we work together.

Will they inspire you too?

William Kamkwamba

Name:	William Kamkwamba
Location:	Wimbe, Malawi
Problem faced:	Drought
Invention:	Wind turbine
Age at the time:	14 years

William Kamkwamba was a curious young boy who loved learning. He spent most of his days at the local library, reading about engineering and science.

When he was fourteen, a terrible drought hit his village. Crops failed, and food supplies ran out. William had to leave school as his family couldn't afford the fees. However, he didn't give up on his dreams.

What did William do?

While reading, William found a book about **wind turbines**. He realized that building his own turbine might power his family's home.

He collected an assortment of scrap materials from around his village and used them to start building his wind turbine.

Many people in his community laughed at him, so William worked in secret.

An assortment is a mixture of different things or people.

Did William's wind turbine work?

After months of hard work and steady determination, William's wind turbine was completed. It <u>exceeded</u> even his expectations. It produced enough electricity to power many lights and charge people's mobile phones.

After William's first turbine was such a success, more were built in his village.

William working on his invention

His success made him a local celebrity. He was invited to lead a science club in his local school.

A few years later, William was visited by a scientist, who invited reporters to see his invention. William was then invited to go back to school and to speak to experts at a **conference**.

At the conference, he shared his inspiring story, and his dream of bringing renewable energy to his village.

To <u>exceed</u> something is to be bigger, better, or more than it.

News of William's invention spread quickly, and he was invited to speak at many events. His story inspired people everywhere.

William received support and advice from different scientists, engineers and renewable energy experts. He used this to improve his design, and built more wind turbines for his community.

As a result of his determination, William's community reduced their dependence on fossil fuel energy sources by **harnessing** wind power. This lowered their carbon emissions by a lot.

William wrote a book about his experience, which was turned into a film called *The Boy Who Harnessed the Wind*.

William at a showing of the film

William's actions <u>represent</u> a worldwide movement towards renewable energy and a cleaner planet.

If one thing is an example of another thing, it can be said to <u>represent</u> the other thing.

Boyan Slat

Name: Boyan Slat

Location: Delft, the Netherlands

Problem faced: Plastic in the ocean

Invention: A machine to remove plastic from the ocean

Age at the time: 16 years

Boyan Slat invented a device that gathers plastic from the ocean.

When he was sixteen, he went diving and saw more plastic than fish. He decided to find a way to solve the problem of plastic pollution.

While he was at school, Boyan started analysing the issue in detail. He discovered it was a dangerous problem for Earth.

Plastic waste in oceans

- 8 million tonnes of plastic waste end up in our oceans every year.

- Animals in the ocean can get tangled up in it.

- They also end up eating it, which can choke or poison them.

You analyse something when you think carefully about it, or look carefully at it, considering each part in detail.

Have you heard of the Great Pacific Garbage Patch?

- The Great Pacific Garbage Patch is the largest collection of ocean plastic in the world.

- It floats in the Pacific Ocean between California and Hawaii.

- It covers an area of 1.6 million square kilometres, which is three times the size of France.

Boyan wanted to find a way to clean up the plastic waste in the oceans. He quickly realized that the problem was too big for one person to solve alone. He knew he needed to develop a new approach.

That's when inspiration struck! Boyan created an organization called 'The Ocean Cleanup'.

What was Boyan's solution?

Boyan decided to build a machine to collect plastic waste. This barrier floats on the ocean's surface. It catches floating plastic, while sealife can swim underneath it.

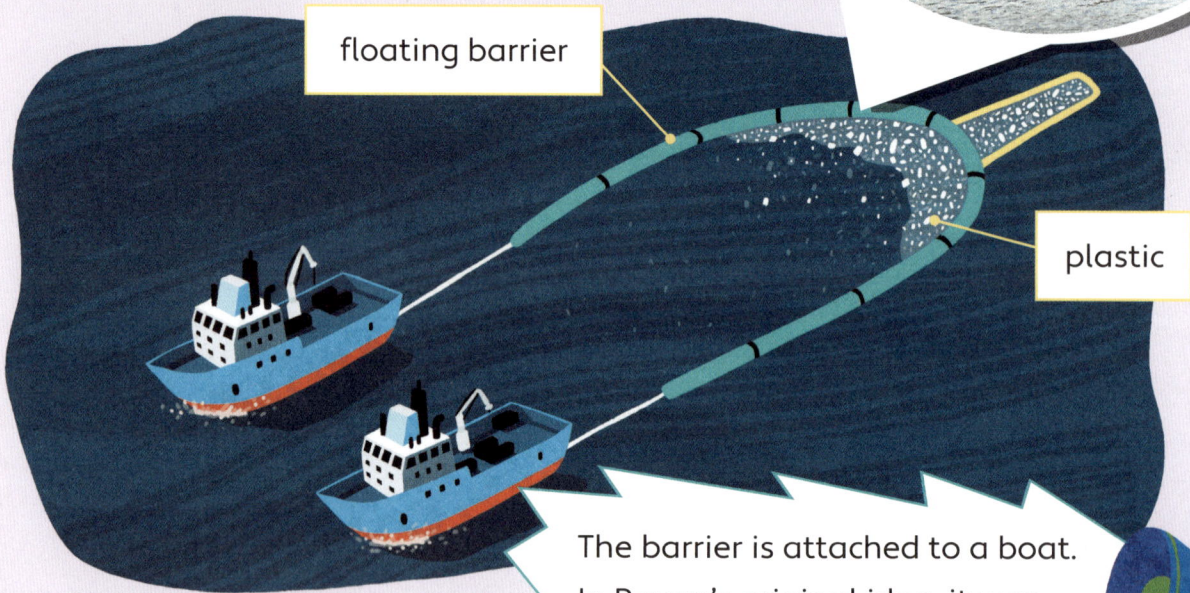

floating barrier

plastic

The barrier is attached to a boat. In Boyan's original idea, it was detached and could float around.

The Ocean Cleanup was even more effective than Boyan expected it to be. His incredible invention gained worldwide attention and Boyan became a hero! After that, he was invited all over the world to speak about the cause and his solution.

Boyan continues to improve his ocean cleaning technology. It has already removed more than 100 000 kilograms of plastic from the ocean.

To detach something is to remove it or separate it.

Small acts for big changes

Boyan's and William's stories show that young people can lead positive change. They can help to create a cleaner, more sustainable future for everyone.

Climate activism is not only about creating innovative solutions to problems, though. It's also about making small, hands-on changes in your daily life.

These small changes can all help the planet:

- recycle and reuse. • plant trees. • don't waste food. • pick up litter.

Imagine if everyone took these small actions every day. The world would transform!

Some young activists have taken small steps that have rippled through their communities and further. They have inspired others to join their cause.

The stories of Lilly Platt and Leah Namugerwa prove just how much impact these actions can have.

Lilly Platt

Name: Lilly Platt

Location: Zeist, the Netherlands

Problem faced: Plastic pollution in her neighbourhood

Invention: Starting 'Lilly's Plastic Pick-Up', which motivated thousands of people

Age at the time: 7 years

Lilly Platt began her fight against plastic pollution at just seven years old. She was born in the United Kingdom, and had just moved to the Netherlands.

One day, she was walking through a local park near her new home. She noticed litter scattered on the ground.

She quickly <u>analysed</u> the situation. It was clear that people were careless with their waste.

She realized how much it was harming the environment. From that moment, Lilly felt a spark of determination.

What did Lilly do?

Lilly started by simply picking up the litter in her park herself. She quickly discovered that her small actions made a huge difference to the park.

You <u>analyse</u> something when you think carefully about it, or look carefully at it, considering each part in detail.

She organized litter-picking events with her family and friends. They began collecting bags of rubbish every week.

Lilly's passion for the environment grew. She knew she had to speak out and inspire more people to help.

As Lilly became more involved, she uncovered an alarming truth. Plastic pollution was an even bigger problem than she had thought.

Impacts of plastic litter

- Plastic takes hundreds of years to break down.

- It harms wildlife, trapping and poisoning animals.

- Plastic bags enter our water system and block drains.

- Chemicals in plastic can leak out and cause problems.

This new knowledge increased Lilly's desire to find solutions to this important issue.

Lilly started talking to her community about making a difference. She campaigned on social media to raise awareness. She used her growing understanding to justify the importance of reducing **single-use plastics**.

To justify something is to show or say that it is right, fair or reasonable.

Lilly's Plastic Pickup

Lilly's small actions inspired more and more people. Large crowds joined her to clean their local beaches and rivers. She even began working with businesses and organizations to reduce plastic waste and promote **sustainability**.

Lilly has been involved with several global organizations, whose work includes:

- making sure that clean water is available to everyone

- reducing the use of plastic

- creating a festival for young people with an eco focus

- running a website that shares stories about climate change.

In just 7 years, Lilly picked up over 300 000 pieces of litter!

Lilly speaks to young people about these issues, and also represents young people's views.

To represent someone is to act or speak on their behalf.

Leah Namugerwa

Name: Leah Namugerwa

Location: Kampala, Uganda

Problem faced: Landslides and deforestation

Invention: Planting trees, which inspired others to do the same

Age at the time: 15 years

Leah's community suffered repeated droughts and flooding, which Leah recognized were caused by climate change.

She decided to take action herself by planting trees. Trees do incredible work for our planet.

Trees shelter many animals.

Their leaves 'clean' the air.

They protect soil from washing away.

How do trees 'clean' the air?

- Trees' leaves absorb carbon dioxide, removing it from the air.

- With energy from the sun, they change parts of this into chemicals they use to grow.

- This process means oxygen is left over. It is released back into the air.

Many trees are cut down to make space for homes and farming. This harms our planet and <u>undermines</u> efforts against climate change.

Tree planting is a powerful environmental tool.

What did Leah do?

Leah wanted to make a difference and help slow climate change. So she started to plant trees. While working, she spoke to young people and adults about ways to care for our planet. News of Leah's work spread quickly.

On her 15th birthday, Leah chose to plant 200 fruit trees instead of having a party. For her 16th birthday, she planted an incredible 500 trees!

To <u>undermine</u> a plan, a person or their efforts is to make them less effective.

Leah's actions, although they started small, made a big difference in her community. She raised awareness about the importance of trees. She also encouraged others to plant trees to celebrate their birthdays.

Leah continues to plant trees and inspire others to follow her lead. Her Birthday Trees project has now grown to include thousands of trees across Uganda. Everywhere they grow, they positively impact the environment.

Leah has spoken at important events all around the world.

Leah has also been recognized for other activist work. She raises awareness about the many actions we need to take to fight climate change, including a campaign to ban plastic bags.

Voices for justice

I hope you found Lilly's and Leah's actions as motivating as I did!

Your voice can be an extraordinary tool to create positive change. There are plenty of different ways to make your voice heard.

Campaigning

- Campaigning is working in an active way towards a particular goal.

- It can include talking to people, organizing events and spreading awareness.

Petitioning

- A petition is a document signed by a lot of people. It asks for a particular thing.

- The number of signatures shows how many people support the idea.

Protesting

- A protest is speech or action **objecting** to something.

- Protests could include any actions, from marches to simply refusing to move.

We'll now discover the stories of Licypriya Kangujam and Jamie Margolin. They've used their voices to fight for climate action.

Licypriya Kangujam

Name:	Licypriya Kangujam
Location:	Bashikhong, India
Problem faced:	Flooding; not enough being done to slow down climate change
Invention:	Using her voice to campaign for climate action
Age at the time:	8 years

Licypriya saw the effects of climate change around her home: floods destroying houses and crops. She knew had to do something to help.

What did Licypriya do?

She spoke out about climate change and its impact on the world. She talked about the importance of educating children about climate change in schools.

Her dedication inspired other children and young people to join her in the fight.

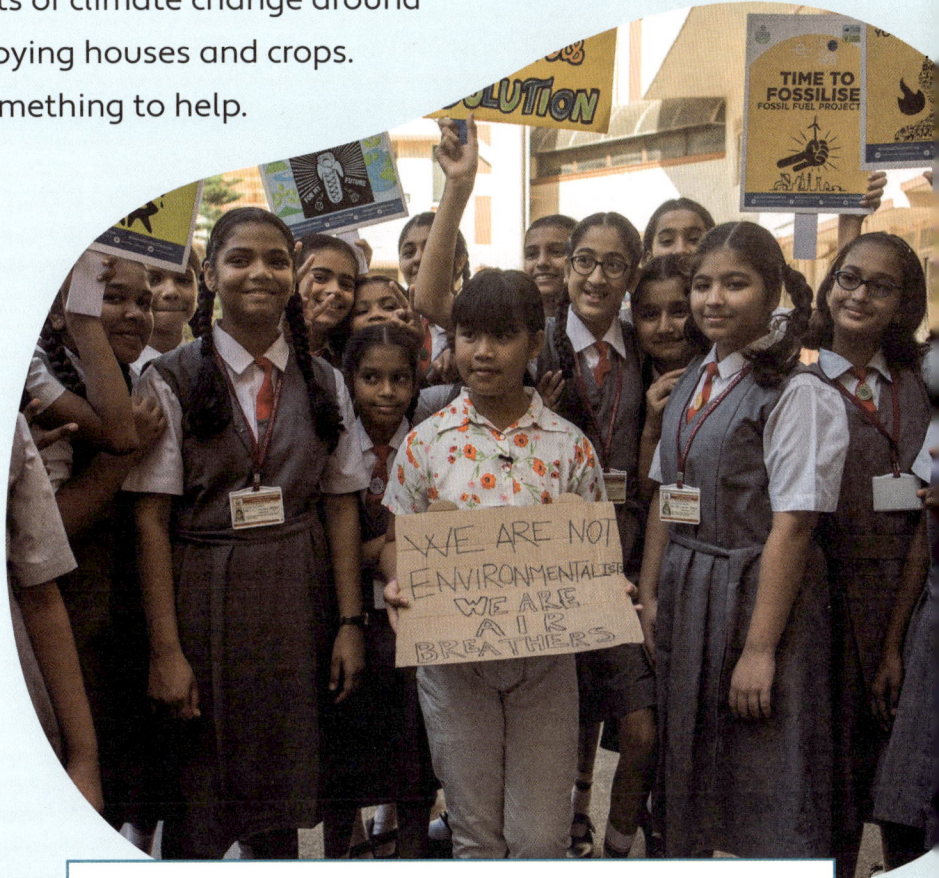

Licypriya gave passionate speeches at schools. She lead projects calling for action on climate change, and the right to breathe clean air.

Licypriya was determined to spread her message further. She attended the United Nations Climate Change Conference in 2019. She became the youngest ever climate activist to speak at the conference – at just eight years old!

What is the United Nations?

- The United Nations was formed in 1945, to help countries solve problems together.

- It brings together leaders from 193 member countries.

- It urges them to work on issues of global importance, like climate change.

Licypriya advised world leaders to take immediate action to slow climate change. She reminded them they had serious responsibilities. They had to create a better place for all the children in the world.

Following the conference, Licypriya united with other activists, including Greta Thunberg. They wrote a newspaper article asking world leaders to stop paying for fossil fuels.

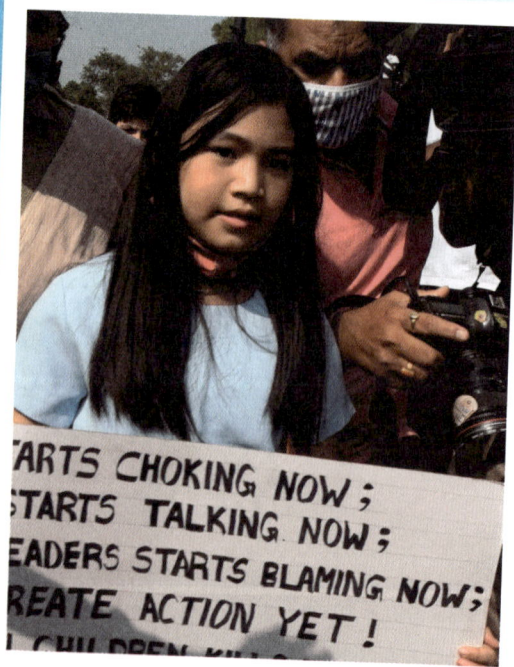

To advise someone is to tell them what you think they should do.

Greta Thunberg

- Greta is a Swedish climate activist born in 2003.

- She began the 'Fridays for Future' protests, sitting by official buildings rather than going to school on Fridays. Thousands of students joined in all over the world.

- Greta has given speeches to world leaders and been nominated for the **Nobel Peace Prize**.

Licypriya's detailed arguments have impressed people across the globe. She explains them with facts and figures, and never allows inaccurate information to weaken her cause.

What can we learn from Licypriya?

Educate yourself on the issues you care about.

Understand the problems, and find solutions that will work for your community.

Act now, instead of waiting for adults to make changes.

No matter how young you are, you can make a difference.

Inaccurate means not correct.

Jamie Margolin

Name:	Jamie Margolin
Location:	Seattle, US
Problem faced:	Adults not doing enough to tackle climate change
Invention:	Setting up 'Zero Hour'
Age at the time:	14 years

Growing up, Jamie became aware of social and environmental issues. She realized that the adults in power weren't doing enough about climate change. She believed young people like her needed to take action.

What did Jamie do?

Jamie created an organization called Zero Hour. It is a group of young people who fight for the planet and support each other.

Through Zero Hour, Jamie has connected with other young activists. They are all passionate about combating climate change.

Jamie has celebrated lots of achievements as an activist. One of the most important was organizing a National Day of Action. It was held in July 2018, when Jamie was just sixteen.

The day's main event was the Youth Climate March. Jamie and her team led thousands of young people in marches across the United States.

Young activists demanded new laws that put climate change solutions in place. They asked the government to take steps to protect all communities.

Jamie has continued to fight for climate justice. She has spoken at many international conferences and events.

Since then, Jamie has written a book about activism. The book encourages young people to let their voices be heard.

Jamie believes that adults in power have hurt future generations' rights to clean air, water and a safe planet. However, she remains hopeful.

If Jamie's story inspires you, then you can learn from what she has done.

Find an issue you're passionate about and research it thoroughly.

You will feel more hopeful if you do something about a problem, instead of waiting for it to be fixed.

Work in a team of people to support each other during this difficult fight for climate action.

People who speak up for change reassure me that there is hope for the future. So do all the other young climate heroes in this book! Do *you* think so, too?

To reassure someone is to say or do something that makes them feel less worried.

Get involved!

Have you found the stories of these young climate activists motivating? I know I have!

Their stories show that you have incredible powers to create change, no matter how old you are. They are proof that one person can make a difference.

Let's follow their lead and take action to create a better world.

How can you do this?

Use your voice and actions to inspire change.

Have confidence in your ability to think of solutions.

Show others that living sustainably is possible.

Remember, anyone can become an activist.

You may prefer to start with your own small actions, or to let your voice be heard. You could use the tips on the next few pages to start your activism adventure!

Small changes: reducing your carbon footprint

One way people can help is by making changes in their own lives to reduce their carbon footprint.

What is a carbon footprint?

Someone's carbon footprint is the amount of carbon dioxide released into the atmosphere by what they do. Reducing our carbon emissions slows climate change and protects our planet.

So, how can people make their carbon footprint smaller?

• Turn off lights when they're not needed.

• Walk, cycle or take public transport if possible, instead of travelling in a car.

• Mend things instead of buying new things.

• Eat more plant-based food.

Bigger changes: helping the natural world around you

There are many ways you can help the planet, and you don't have to help the *whole* planet all at once! Perhaps you could start by helping nature near where you live?

You could …

Ask an adult if there is somewhere you can plant a tree, like Leah.

Ask your teacher if you can help to make your school a greener place.

Ask an adult about going on a litter pick, like Lilly.

There is no action too big or small. Think about what's important to you and what you can do near where you live.

What's the problem with plastic?

Plastic is a useful material. It is light and it can be made into lots of different shapes. However, making plastic releases lots of carbon dioxide. When plastic is thrown away, it is bad for the environment.

Ways people can reduce plastic:

- carrying reusable water bottles
- carrying reusable shopping bags
- using plastic things for as long as possible before replacing them.

The biggest change: using your voice

You may decide you'd like to speak up on bigger issues. You could talk to people about climate change, like Licypriya did. Inspired by Jamie, you could ask an adult to help you write to an important person about climate change. You could be a hero of renewable energy, like William.

What is renewable energy?

Renewable energy comes from natural sources like the sun, wind and water. Unlike fossil fuels, these will never run out and don't release carbon.

As we've seen together, every action could lead to change. So, if you're passionate about an issue and want to make a difference, get involved.

You never know what kind of impact you'll make on the world!

Glossary

Artificial intelligence (AI): a computer's ability to use reasoning, learning, planning and creativity

atmosphere: layer of gases surrounding Earth

carbon dioxide: a gas that forms part of the atmosphere and can trap heat around Earth

conference: large formal meeting in which people discuss a specific subject

emissions: substances (usually gases) that are produced and let out

fossil fuels: fuels (things that can be burned for energy) that were created underground over millions of years: coal, oil and natural gas

harnessing: controlling something and making use of it

impact: a strong influence or effect

innovative: new and original, usually based on intelligence and creativity

Nobel Peace Prize: prize that is usually awarded once a year for an outstanding contribution to peace

objecting: saying that something is wrong

single-use plastics: plastic objects that are used only once and then thrown away

sustainability: ability to keep going in the same way

wind turbines: machines that can create electricity when a part of them is moved around and around by the wind

Index